# Capricorn Horoscope 2025

By
Thalia C. Astraea

# Table of Contents
# Capricorn (Dec. 22 – Jan. 19)

# Personality

**Capricorn** (December 22 – January 19), symbolized by the Goat, is an Earth sign ruled by Saturn. Known for their discipline, ambition, and practicality, Capricorns are determined achievers who excel at turning dreams into reality. They value tradition, structure, and long-term success, making them reliable and focused individuals.

**Core Traits of Capricorn**

1. **Ambitious and Goal-Oriented:** Capricorns set high standards for themselves and work diligently to achieve their goals, no matter how challenging.
2. **Practical and Disciplined:** They approach life with a grounded and realistic perspective, excelling at planning and executing their objectives.
3. **Responsible and Dependable:** Capricorns take their commitments seriously and can be counted on to fulfill their responsibilities.
4. **Patient and Resilient:** They understand the value of perseverance and are willing to put in the time and effort required for success.
5. **Wise and Thoughtful:** With Saturn's influence, Capricorns often have a mature and reflective nature, allowing them to make sound decisions.

## Strengths of Capricorn

- **Determination:** Capricorns are persistent and unwavering in the pursuit of their goals.
- **Organizational Skills:** They excel at planning, structuring, and managing both personal and professional projects.
- **Reliability:** Their dependable nature makes them trusted friends, partners, and colleagues.
- **Practical Wisdom:** Capricorns often offer sound advice and insights based on careful consideration and experience.
- **Self-Control:** They are disciplined and able to delay gratification for long-term success.

## Weaknesses of Capricorn

- **Workaholic Tendencies:** Their drive for success can lead to neglecting personal relationships or self-care.
- **Pessimism:** Capricorns may sometimes focus too much on obstacles, which can dampen their optimism.
- **Overly Serious:** Their serious demeanor can make them seem unapproachable or overly rigid.
- **Stubbornness:** Once they set their minds on something, they may resist change or alternate perspectives.

- **Fear of Failure:** Their high standards can lead to self-doubt or fear of falling short.

**Capricorn in Relationships**

*As Partners:*

Capricorns are loyal, committed, and supportive in relationships. They seek stability and are most compatible with partners who share their values and long-term vision.

- **Strengths in Love:** Capricorns are devoted, dependable, and deeply caring, often showing their love through actions rather than words.
- **Challenges in Love:** They may struggle with vulnerability, focusing more on practicality than emotional expression.

*As Friends:*

Capricorns are reliable and trustworthy friends who value meaningful connections over superficial interactions. They are excellent listeners and provide sound advice.

- **Strengths in Friendship:** Loyal, wise, and supportive, they are always there when needed.

- **Challenges in Friendship:** Their work-focused nature may sometimes limit their social availability.

*As Family Members:*

Capricorns are dedicated and responsible family members, often taking on leadership roles within the family and providing stability.

## Capricorn in Career and Professional Life

Capricorns thrive in careers that value discipline, structure, and results. They excel in roles that require leadership, strategy, and long-term planning.

*Ideal Career Paths:*

- **Business or Finance:** Their practical mindset and organizational skills make them natural leaders in these fields.
- **Engineering or Architecture:** Capricorns excel in careers that require precision, planning, and execution.
- **Law or Politics:** Their dedication to rules and systems aligns well with roles involving governance or advocacy.

- **Healthcare or Science:** Capricorns' disciplined and analytical nature makes them great in research or medical fields.
- **Education or Mentorship:** Their wisdom and patience allow them to guide and inspire others effectively.

*Workplace Traits:*

- **Strengths:** Hardworking, reliable, and strategic, Capricorns bring a focused and goal-oriented approach to their work.
- **Challenges:** They may struggle with delegating tasks or balancing work with personal life.

## Capricorn and Personal Growth

To reach their full potential, Capricorns can benefit from learning to balance their ambitious nature with emotional openness and self-care.

*Tips for Personal Growth:*

1. **Embrace Vulnerability:** Practice expressing emotions and building deeper personal connections.
2. **Balance Work and Play:** Schedule time for relaxation and leisure to maintain overall well-being.

3. **Stay Optimistic:** Focus on possibilities rather than limitations to cultivate a positive mindset.
4. **Be Flexible:** Adapt to change and be open to alternate perspectives to enhance problem-solving.
5. **Celebrate Success:** Take time to acknowledge and appreciate your achievements, no matter how small.

## Capricorn Compatibility

- **Best Matches:** Taurus, Virgo, Scorpio, and Pisces—these signs appreciate Capricorn's stability, dedication, and reliability.
- **Challenging Matches:** Aries and Gemini, whose spontaneous and free-spirited natures may clash with Capricorn's disciplined and structured approach.

## Conclusion

Capricorns are ambitious, dependable, and practical individuals who excel at achieving their goals and providing stability to those around them. While their disciplined nature is a key strength, they can enhance their lives by embracing flexibility, emotional expression, and work-life balance. With their unwavering determination and wisdom, Capricorns have the potential to create a fulfilling and successful life for themselves and their loved ones.

# Introduce

Capricorn (December 22 – January 19), 2025 is poised to be a year of transformative growth and significant milestones. With your ruling planet, Saturn, influencing key areas of life and the presence of other powerful celestial alignments, you will experience a unique combination of challenges and opportunities. Known for your discipline, ambition, and practicality, you're well-equipped to navigate these shifts and emerge stronger and more focused than ever.

In 2025, themes of personal transformation, professional growth, and emotional connection will take center stage. This year encourages you to balance your steadfast determination with adaptability and a willingness to embrace new perspectives. By focusing on building strong foundations and nurturing meaningful relationships, you'll create a path that aligns with your long-term goals and values.

**Overall Energy for Capricorn in 2025**

The year begins with Jupiter in Taurus, a fellow Earth sign, creating a supportive and harmonious energy for Capricorn. This placement emphasizes creativity, financial growth, and stability, making it an excellent time to focus on building your resources and pursuing personal or professional projects. Jupiter's energy also enhances your ability to take calculated risks and reap the rewards of your hard work.

Saturn in Pisces continues to influence your communication, self-expression, and relationships. This transit encourages you to be more open emotionally and to deepen your connections with others. It's a period of reflection, allowing you to address past challenges and emerge with greater emotional clarity and resilience.

Later in the year, when Jupiter moves into Gemini, the focus shifts to adaptability, learning, and collaboration. This dynamic energy will inspire you to expand your horizons, develop new skills, and embrace innovative approaches to problem-solving. The combination of these planetary influences ensures a year of steady growth and meaningful achievements.

## Career and Ambition

2025 is a standout year for Capricorns in terms of professional growth and achievement. With Jupiter in Taurus during the first half of the year, you'll experience a period of stability and expansion in your career. This is an excellent time to focus on long-term goals, refine your skills, and take on leadership roles.

As Jupiter transitions into Gemini mid-year, the pace quickens, bringing opportunities to collaborate, network, and explore new career paths. Your ability to adapt and think outside the box will be a key asset during this time. Saturn in Pisces encourages clear communication, making it a favorable year for presenting ideas, negotiating deals, and building strong professional relationships.

- **Key Opportunities:** Promotions, entrepreneurial ventures, and creative projects will shine in 2025.
- **Challenges:** Balancing your need for structure with the flexibility required to navigate unexpected changes.

**Tips for Career Success in 2025:**

1. Focus on strategic planning during the first half of the year to build a strong foundation for future growth.
2. Embrace collaborative efforts and networking opportunities in the latter half of the year.
3. Stay open to learning and adapting to new technologies or approaches.

## Finance and Wealth

Financially, 2025 offers stability and potential growth for Capricorn. Jupiter in Taurus emphasizes disciplined financial planning and rewards for past investments or efforts. This is an ideal time to focus on saving, investing, and building wealth for the future.

When Jupiter moves into Gemini, new income opportunities may arise through side projects, collaborations, or intellectual pursuits. However, it's essential to remain cautious and avoid impulsive financial decisions during this time.

- **Key Opportunities:** Steady income growth, successful investments, and financial stability will define the year.
- **Challenges:** Balancing ambition with financial prudence and resisting the urge to take unnecessary risks.

**Tips for Financial Success in 2025:**

1. Stick to a disciplined budget and prioritize saving for long-term goals.
2. Explore opportunities to diversify your income sources, particularly during Gemini season.
3. Seek professional advice for major investments or financial decisions.

## Love and Relationships

Relationships take on greater depth and significance for Capricorn in 2025. Saturn in Pisces encourages emotional openness and vulnerability, allowing you to connect more deeply with loved ones. This is a year to strengthen existing bonds, heal past wounds, and build trust in your relationships.

For singles, Jupiter's influence in Gemini later in the year creates opportunities to meet new people through social activities, travel, or intellectual pursuits. Emotional compatibility and shared values will play a key role in forming meaningful connections.

- **For Singles:** The first half of the year is ideal for self-reflection and understanding your needs in a partner. Mid-year brings exciting opportunities for romantic connections.
- **For Those in Relationships:** Focus on nurturing trust, communication, and shared goals with your partner. Late 2025 is a favorable time for resolving conflicts and deepening your bond.

## Challenges in Love:

- Balancing your work commitments with personal relationships.

- Letting go of past fears or doubts that may hinder emotional growth.

**Tips for Love and Relationships in 2025:**

1. Practice active listening and empathy to strengthen emotional connections.
2. Be patient and open to vulnerability, allowing deeper trust to develop.
3. Celebrate small moments of joy and appreciation in your relationships.

**Health and Wellness**

Health is a key focus for Capricorn in 2025, with Saturn encouraging balance and self-discipline. This is a year to refine your wellness routines, focusing on sustainable habits that support both physical and mental well-being.

The first half of the year is ideal for building strength and resilience through regular exercise, mindful eating, and stress management. As the pace picks up in the latter half of the year, prioritize relaxation and self-care to avoid burnout.

- **Physical Health:** Focus on grounding practices like yoga, walking, or strength training to maintain vitality.

- **Mental and Emotional Health:** Embrace reflective practices like journaling or meditation to manage stress and gain clarity.

## Challenges in Health:

- Overworking or neglecting self-care during busy periods.
- Managing stress or emotional tension caused by work or personal responsibilities.

## Tips for Health and Wellness in 2025:

1. Create a balanced routine that includes exercise, relaxation, and mindfulness.
2. Avoid pushing yourself too hard and listen to your body's signals.
3. Dedicate time to hobbies or creative outlets that bring joy and relaxation.

## Personal Growth and Spirituality

2025 is a year of profound personal growth and transformation for Capricorn. Saturn in Pisces encourages introspection, helping you release limiting beliefs and embrace a more compassionate and open perspective.

Pluto's transit into Aquarius fuels your desire for innovation and self-improvement, inspiring you to explore new ideas, technologies, or philosophies. This is a year to align with your authentic self and create a life that reflects your values and aspirations.

**Key Themes:**

- Emotional growth, self-reflection, and building resilience.
- Exploring new areas of learning, creativity, and spirituality.

**Tips for Personal Growth in 2025:**

1. Trust your instincts and embrace opportunities for change.
2. Surround yourself with people who support and inspire your growth.
3. Celebrate your achievements and acknowledge the progress you've made.

**Key Dates for Capricorn in 2025**

- **March 14:** A New Moon in Pisces highlights emotional growth and creative endeavors.
- **May 17:** A Full Moon in Scorpio brings clarity to your goals and inspires transformation.
- **October 12:** A New Moon in Libra encourages balance and harmony in relationships.

## Challenges for Capricorn in 2025

- Balancing your ambitious nature with emotional openness and self-care.
- Managing stress during periods of intense work or change.
- Letting go of rigid structures to embrace adaptability and new opportunities.

## Conclusion

2025 is a year of growth, transformation, and achievement for Capricorn. By embracing emotional openness, focusing on meaningful connections, and maintaining balance in your personal and professional life, you'll navigate this transformative year with confidence and purpose.

Capricorn, the road ahead is filled with opportunities—this is your time to shine and create a life that aligns with your highest aspirations.

# January

January 2025 is a month of focus, ambition, and groundwork for Capricorn. With the Sun in your sign for most of the month, the energy supports setting clear goals, refining your plans, and taking decisive steps toward your long-term ambitions. This is a powerful time for personal growth, professional advancement, and building a solid foundation for the rest of the year.

## *Work*

January emphasizes productivity and strategic planning in Capricorn's professional life.

- **Opportunities:** Capricorn Energy supports tackling complex projects, setting realistic goals, and demonstrating leadership skills. Mid-month, opportunities may arise to take on new responsibilities or showcase your expertise.
- **Challenges:** Avoid being overly critical of yourself or others as you push toward perfection. Maintain patience with slower processes.

**Advice:** Use this month to prioritize tasks, focus on consistent progress, and align your efforts with your long-term vision.

## *Finance*

Your financial outlook in January highlights stability and careful planning.

- **Opportunities:** This is a favorable time to reassess your budget, focus on saving, and explore ways to grow your wealth. Rewards may come from disciplined financial habits established in the past.
- **Challenges:** Avoid unnecessary expenses or impulsive purchases, especially on luxury items.

**Advice:** Stick to a realistic financial plan and prioritize long-term stability over short-term indulgence.

## *Love*

January brings warmth and stability to Capricorn's love life.

- **For Singles:** Reflect on your relationship goals and take your time building connections. Someone with shared values may come into your life through work or mutual interests.
- **For Those in Relationships:** Focus on strengthening communication and creating stability with your partner. Thoughtful gestures and meaningful conversations will deepen your bond.

**Advice:** Be patient and authentic in your interactions. Use this time to nurture emotional stability and trust in your relationships.

## *Health*

Health-wise, January encourages Capricorn to maintain consistency and balance.

- **Strengths:** The Capricorn energy supports building healthy routines that enhance both physical and mental well-being. Activities like yoga, meditation, or regular exercise will help you stay grounded.
- **Challenges:** Overworking or neglecting rest may affect your energy levels if not managed properly.

**Advice:** Incorporate relaxation techniques into your routine. Focus on maintaining a balanced diet, staying hydrated, and getting adequate sleep.

## Be Careful

- **Overworking:** Avoid overloading yourself with responsibilities, as this could lead to burnout.
- **Stubbornness:** Be open to feedback and alternate perspectives in work and personal matters.
- **Neglecting Self-Care:** Balance your ambition with rest to maintain overall well-being.

## Advice

1. **Plan Strategically:** Use Capricorn's disciplined energy to set clear and achievable goals for the year.
2. **Nurture Relationships:** Focus on building trust and stability in your personal and professional connections.
3. **Practice Balance:** Maintain harmony by dedicating time to both your ambitions and self-care.

## Additional Tips

- **Lucky Days:** January 10, 15, and 28 – Ideal for decision-making, creative pursuits, or strengthening relationships.
- **Lucky Color:** Forest Green – This color symbolizes grounding, growth, and balance.
- **Affirmation for January:** *"I align my actions with my purpose, creating stability and success in all areas of my life."*

January 2025 is a month of focus and preparation for Capricorn. By concentrating on meaningful goals, disciplined planning, and self-care, you'll set the stage for a productive and fulfilling year ahead.

# February

February 2025 is a month of creativity, connection, and thoughtful planning for Capricorn. With the Sun in Aquarius for most of the month, the focus shifts to innovation, social engagement, and expanding your ideas. As the Sun transitions into Pisces later in February, the energy becomes more introspective and emotional, encouraging you to reflect on your goals and nurture meaningful connections.

## _Work_

February emphasizes collaboration and innovation in Capricorn's professional life.

- **Opportunities:** The Aquarius energy supports brainstorming, team projects, and exploring fresh ideas for solving problems. Late in the month, Pisces' influence inspires creativity and intuitive decision-making, making it a great time for tackling complex tasks or refining your vision.
- **Challenges:** Avoid being too rigid in your approach, as flexibility and adaptability will be key to making the most of this dynamic energy.

**Advice:** Use Aquarius energy to collaborate and think outside the box, and Pisces energy to align your plans with your inner values.

## _Finance_

Your financial outlook in February highlights balance and careful planning.

- **Opportunities:** Financial rewards may come from collaborative efforts, creative ventures, or innovative solutions to existing challenges.
- **Challenges:** Avoid impulsive spending or taking unnecessary risks, especially during moments of high energy or excitement.

**Advice:** Stick to a disciplined budget and focus on saving for long-term goals. Consider seeking advice before making significant financial decisions.

## _Love_

February brings warmth and connection to Capricorn's love life.

- **For Singles:** Romantic opportunities may arise through work, social gatherings, or shared interests. Aquarius energy fosters intellectual connections, while Pisces energy later in the month adds emotional depth.
- **For Those in Relationships:** Focus on strengthening communication and creating meaningful experiences with your partner. Late

February is ideal for rekindling romance and deepening emotional intimacy.

**Advice:** Be open and authentic in your interactions. Use Aquarius energy to keep things lively and Pisces energy to nurture emotional bonds.

## *Health*

Health-wise, February encourages Capricorn to focus on mental and emotional well-being.

- **Strengths:** The Aquarius energy supports staying active and engaging in activities that stimulate both the body and mind. Late in the month, Pisces' influence promotes relaxation and emotional healing.
- **Challenges:** Stress from juggling work and personal responsibilities may affect your energy levels if not managed properly.

**Advice:** Incorporate relaxation techniques like meditation or journaling into your daily routine. Focus on maintaining a balanced diet, staying hydrated, and ensuring you get enough rest to recharge.

# Be Careful

- **Overcommitting:** Avoid taking on too many responsibilities, as this could lead to stress or burnout.
- **Impulsiveness:** Think carefully before making major decisions in work or financial matters.
- **Neglecting Self-Care:** Balance your active schedule with downtime to maintain overall well-being.

# Advice

1. **Think Creatively:** Use Aquarius energy to explore innovative solutions and new perspectives.
2. **Reflect and Nurture:** Embrace Pisces' influence to align your actions with your values and strengthen your relationships.
3. **Stay Grounded:** Maintain consistency in your wellness routines and prioritize balance in all areas of your life.

# Additional Tips

- **Lucky Days:** February 8, 16, and 27 – Perfect for networking, decision-making, or fostering meaningful relationships.

- **Lucky Color:** Light Blue – This color symbolizes clarity, inspiration, and harmony.
- **Affirmation for February:** *"I balance creativity with practicality, creating harmony and growth in my life."*

February 2025 is a month of dynamic energy and meaningful progress for Capricorn. By focusing on collaboration, thoughtful planning, and self-care, you'll navigate this vibrant period with clarity and confidence.

# March

March 2025 is a month of introspection, creativity, and preparation for Capricorn. With the Sun in Pisces for most of the month, the energy encourages emotional depth, imaginative pursuits, and nurturing meaningful relationships. As the Sun transitions into Aries later in March, the focus shifts to action, ambition, and laying the groundwork for future goals. This combination of introspection and dynamic energy makes March a transformative and fulfilling time.

## *Work*

March emphasizes creativity and strategic action in Capricorn's professional life.

- **Opportunities:** Pisces Energy supports innovative thinking and refining your plans. Late in the month, Aries' influence inspires bold moves, making it an excellent time to take decisive action or pursue leadership roles.
- **Challenges:** Balancing your practical mindset with Pisces' dreamy energy may feel challenging. Avoid overanalyzing or hesitating when opportunities arise.

**Advice:** Use Pisces' reflective energy to refine your strategies and Aries' bold energy to execute them with confidence.

## *Finance*

Your financial outlook in March highlights cautious growth and planning.

- **Opportunities:** Financial gains may come from creative projects, side ventures, or investments in areas aligned with your values.
- **Challenges:** Avoid impulsive spending or taking financial risks without thorough research, especially during Aries season's bold energy.

**Advice:** Stick to a disciplined budget and focus on saving for long-term goals. Seek professional advice if considering major financial decisions.

## *Love*

March brings warmth and connection to Capricorn's love life, with Venus enhancing harmony and emotional depth.

- **For Singles:** Romantic opportunities may arise through creative activities, travel, or social events.

Pisces' influence encourages emotional compatibility and meaningful conversations.

- **For Those in Relationships:** Focus on strengthening emotional intimacy and building trust with your partner. Late March is perfect for planning adventures or celebrating your connection.

**Advice:** Be open and present in your interactions. Use Pisces' nurturing energy to deepen bonds and Aries' dynamic spirit to keep things lively.

### *Health*

Health-wise, March encourages Capricorn to focus on balance and energy management.

- **Strengths:** Pisces energy supports mindfulness practices like meditation, yoga, or creative outlets that promote relaxation. Aries' influence later in the month boosts physical vitality and motivation.
- **Challenges:** Stress from juggling responsibilities may affect your energy levels if not managed effectively.

**Advice:** Maintain consistency in your wellness routines. Prioritize relaxation and physical activity, and ensure you're staying hydrated and eating balanced meals.

- **Overthinking:** Avoid second-guessing yourself or overanalyzing situations. Trust your instincts and take calculated risks when needed.
- **Neglecting Rest:** Balance your active schedule with adequate downtime to maintain overall well-being.
- **Impulsiveness:** Think carefully before making major decisions, particularly in financial or professional matters.

## Advice

1. **Reflect and Refine:** Use Pisces' influence to align your goals with your values and nurture meaningful connections.
2. **Take Bold Action:** Embrace Aries' energy to step into leadership roles and pursue opportunities with confidence.
3. **Maintain Balance:** Prioritize self-care and relaxation to sustain your energy and clarity throughout the month.

## Additional Tips

- **Lucky Days:** March 9, 18, and 27 — Ideal for decision-making, creative pursuits, or strengthening relationships.

- **Lucky Color:** Sea Green – This color symbolizes harmony, balance, and renewal.
- **Affirmation for March:** *"I balance reflection with bold action, creating harmony and growth in all areas of my life."*

March 2025 is a month of introspection and empowerment for Capricorn. By focusing on meaningful connections, thoughtful planning, and dynamic action, you'll navigate this transformative period with confidence and clarity.

# April

April 2025 is a month of action, focus, and progress for Capricorn. With the Sun in Aries for most of the month, the energy encourages ambition, leadership, and bold decision-making. As the Sun transitions into Taurus later in April, the focus shifts toward stability, grounding, and refining your goals. This combination of fiery momentum and practical grounding makes April a productive and rewarding time.

## *Work*

April emphasizes leadership and initiative in Capricorn's professional life.

- **Opportunities:** Aries energy supports stepping into leadership roles, launching new projects, or pursuing bold career moves. Late in the month, Taurus' influence helps you focus on sustainability, making it a great time to refine plans and ensure long-term success.
- **Challenges:** Avoid rushing decisions or becoming overly competitive in Aries' high-energy atmosphere. Balance ambition with practicality.

**Advice:** Use Aries' dynamic energy to take action and Taurus' steady influence to solidify your progress.

<u>*Finance*</u>

Your financial outlook in April highlights growth and careful planning.

- **Opportunities:** Financial rewards may come from bold initiatives, creative ventures, or promotions. This is also a favorable time to reassess your budget and align your spending with your long-term goals.
- **Challenges:** Avoid impulsive spending, especially during moments of excitement or stress.

**Advice:** Focus on saving and thoughtful investments. Use Taurus' practical energy to make informed financial decisions.

<u>*Love*</u>

April brings passion and connection to Capricorn's love life.

- **For Singles:** This is a great time to meet someone new, particularly through social events, work, or shared hobbies. Aries's energy encourages confidence, making it easy to form connections.
- **For Those in Relationships:** Focus on rekindling passion and celebrating your bond with your

partner. Late April is ideal for nurturing emotional stability and planning special moments together.

**Advice:** Be open and attentive in your relationships. Use Aries' adventurous energy to keep things exciting and Taurus' grounding influence to deepen trust and intimacy.

## *Health*

Health-wise, April encourages Capricorn to maintain energy and focus on self-care.

- **Strengths:** Aries energy supports physical activity and motivation, making it a great time to enhance your fitness routine. Taurus' influence later in the month encourages relaxation and grounding practices.
- **Challenges:** Overexertion or neglecting rest during Aries' high-energy period may lead to fatigue if not managed carefully.

**Advice:** Incorporate relaxation techniques into your routine. Focus on maintaining a balanced diet, staying hydrated, and ensuring you get adequate sleep.

<u>*Be Careful*</u>

- **Impulsiveness:** Avoid making hasty decisions, especially in work or financial matters. Take time to evaluate your options.
- **Overworking:** Don't take on too many responsibilities at once, as this could lead to stress or burnout.
- **Neglecting Details:** While focusing on big-picture goals, pay attention to finer details, particularly as the Taurus season begins.

<u>*Advice*</u>

1. **Take Bold Steps:** Use Aries' energy to embrace opportunities and take decisive action on your goals.
2. **Ground Your Efforts:** As Taurus season begins, focus on aligning your actions with your long-term vision and building stability.
3. **Nurture Relationships:** Strengthen bonds with loved ones through meaningful gestures and thoughtful communication.

<u>*Additional Tips*</u>

- **Lucky Days:** April 10, 18, and 27 — Ideal for decision-making, creative pursuits, or strengthening relationships.

- **Lucky Color:** Scarlet Red – This color symbolizes passion, vitality, and confidence.
- **Affirmation for April:** *"I take bold action and align my efforts with my purpose, creating harmony and success in all areas of my life."*

April 2025 is a month of empowerment and progress for Capricorn. By focusing on ambitious goals, thoughtful planning, and meaningful connections, you'll make the most of this dynamic and fulfilling period.

# May

May 2025 is a month of balance, introspection, and steady progress for Capricorn. With the Sun in Taurus for most of the month, the energy emphasizes stability, long-term planning, and building a strong foundation in both personal and professional life. As the Sun transitions into Gemini later in May, the focus shifts to communication, adaptability, and exploring new ideas. This combination of grounded practicality and intellectual curiosity makes May a productive and enriching time.

## *Work*

May emphasizes stability and collaboration in Capricorn's professional life.

- **Opportunities:** Taurus Energy supports completing ongoing projects, building strong professional relationships, and creating sustainable strategies for future growth. Late in the month, Gemini's influence inspires fresh ideas, making it an excellent time to network, brainstorm, and embrace dynamic opportunities.
- **Challenges:** Avoid becoming too rigid in your approach, as adaptability will be key to navigating Gemini's fast-paced energy.

**Advice:** Use Taurus' steady energy to solidify your plans and Gemini's innovative energy to explore new possibilities.

## *Finance*

Your financial outlook in May highlights stability and thoughtful management.

- **Opportunities:** Financial rewards may come from careful budgeting, long-term investments, or new income opportunities through collaborative efforts.
- **Challenges:** Avoid overspending on luxuries or impulsive purchases, particularly during moments of excitement in Gemini season.

**Advice:** Focus on saving and aligning your financial goals with your long-term vision. Consider seeking advice for major financial decisions.

## *Love*

May brings warmth and connection to Capricorn's love life, with Venus enhancing emotional stability and harmony.

- **For Singles:** Romantic opportunities may arise through work, shared activities, or social events. Taurus energy encourages meaningful connections, while Gemini's influence later in the month brings playful and exciting interactions.

- **For Those in Relationships:** Focus on building trust and creating stability with your partner. Late May is perfect for planning fun outings or having deep, meaningful conversations about your shared future.

**Advice:** Be open and genuine in your relationships. Use Taurus energy to nurture emotional stability and Gemini energy to keep things lively and fresh.

## *Health*

Health-wise, May encourages Capricorn to focus on balance and maintaining consistent routines.

- **Strengths:** Taurus energy supports grounding practices like yoga, meditation, or spending time in nature to promote relaxation and resilience. Late in the month, Gemini's influence inspires physical activity and social engagement that boost your overall well-being.
- **Challenges:** Overindulgence or stress from juggling responsibilities may affect your energy levels if not managed effectively.

**Advice:** Prioritize self-care, maintain a healthy diet, and ensure you're getting adequate rest. Incorporate both relaxation and physical activity into your routine.

## *Be Careful*

- **Overindulgence:** Avoid overspending or indulging in unhealthy habits, particularly during social events or celebrations.
- **Neglecting Adaptability:** While focusing on stability, remain open to new ideas and opportunities.
- **Impatience:** Balance your long-term goals with realistic timelines to avoid frustration.

## *Advice*

1. **Focus on Foundations:** Use Taurus energy to create stability in your work, finances, and relationships.
2. **Stay Curious:** Embrace Gemini's influence to explore new opportunities, ideas, and connections.

**Maintain Balance:** Ensure harmony between your responsibilities, self-care, and personal relationships.

<u>*Additional Tips*</u>

- **Lucky Days:** May 11, 18, and 27 – Ideal for decision-making, networking, or creative pursuits.
- **Lucky Color:** Emerald Green – This color symbolizes growth, renewal, and balance.
- **Affirmation for May:** *"I build stability and embrace new opportunities, aligning my actions with my highest purpose."*

May 2025 is a month of grounding and exploration for Capricorn. By focusing on thoughtful planning, meaningful connections, and balanced self-care, you'll navigate this productive period with clarity and confidence.

# June

June 2025 is a month of adaptability, curiosity, and steady growth for Capricorn. With the Sun in Gemini for most of the month, the energy emphasizes communication, networking, and expanding your knowledge. As the Sun transitions into Cancer later in June, the focus shifts to emotional depth, nurturing relationships, and creating a sense of balance between work and personal life. This mix of dynamic interaction and introspection makes June a productive and enriching time for Capricorn.

## *Work*

June emphasizes communication and innovation in Capricorn's professional life.

- **Opportunities:** Gemini Energy supports networking, brainstorming, and collaborating on projects that require fresh ideas. Late in the month, Cancer's influence encourages nurturing workplace relationships and focusing on long-term strategies.
- **Challenges:** Balancing Gemini's fast-paced energy with Cancer's emotional depth may feel challenging. Avoid overanalyzing or procrastinating on decisions.

**Advice:** Use Gemini's dynamic energy to explore new ideas and Cancer's intuitive influence to align your work with your values and goals.

## *Finance*

Your financial outlook in June highlights adaptability and strategic planning.

- **Opportunities:** Financial gains may come from creative endeavors, collaborations, or intellectual pursuits. This is a good time to reassess your budget and prioritize savings for future goals.
- **Challenges:** Avoid impulsive spending, especially during moments of social excitement or emotional highs.

**Advice:** Stick to a disciplined financial plan and focus on aligning your spending with your long-term priorities. Consider seeking advice for significant financial decisions.

## *Love*

June brings warmth and emotional connection to Capricorn's love life, with Venus enhancing harmony and intimacy.

- **For Singles:** Romantic opportunities may arise through social gatherings, intellectual pursuits, or shared hobbies. Gemini energy fosters exciting and lively conversations, while Cancer's influence later in the month deepens emotional bonds.

- **For Those in Relationships:** Focus on open communication and shared experiences with your partner. Late June is ideal for nurturing trust and planning meaningful moments together.

**Advice:** Be present and attentive in your interactions. Use Gemini's lighthearted energy to keep things fun and Cancer's depth to strengthen your connection.

## *Health*

Health-wise, June encourages Capricorn to balance activity with relaxation for overall well-being.

- **Strengths:** Gemini energy supports staying active and engaging in activities that stimulate both body and mind. Late in the month, Cancer's influence promotes emotional healing and self-care practices.
- **Challenges:** Stress from juggling responsibilities may affect your energy levels if not managed properly.

**Advice:** Incorporate mindfulness techniques into your daily routine. Focus on maintaining consistency in your fitness and nutrition, and prioritize rest to recharge.

### _Be Careful_

- **Overcommitting:** Avoid taking on too many responsibilities or social engagements, as this could lead to stress or burnout.
- **Neglecting Details:** Balance your big-picture focus with attention to finer points, especially in work and financial matters.
- **Emotional Overload:** Practice self-awareness to manage emotions and avoid misunderstandings in relationships.

### _Advice_

1. **Stay Open-Minded:** Use Gemini's influence to explore new ideas and expand your horizons through learning and networking.
2. **Nurture Connections:** Embrace Cancer's energy to deepen relationships and prioritize meaningful interactions.
3. **Prioritize Balance:** Maintain harmony by balancing your responsibilities with relaxation and personal well-being.

### _Additional Tips_

- **Lucky Days:** June 8, 16, and 25 – Ideal for decision-making, networking, or creative pursuits.

- **Lucky Color:** Light Blue – This color symbolizes clarity, inspiration, and calmness.
- **Affirmation for June:** *"I balance exploration with introspection, creating harmony and growth in my life."*

June 2025 is a month of communication and connection for Capricorn. By focusing on thoughtful planning, meaningful relationships, and self-care, you'll navigate this dynamic period with confidence and clarity.

# July

July 2025 is a month of emotional connection, self-reflection, and personal growth for Capricorn. With the Sun in Cancer for most of the month, the focus is on nurturing your inner self, strengthening relationships, and creating emotional stability. As the Sun transitions into Leo later in July, the energy shifts toward bold self-expression, ambition, and creative pursuits. This blend of introspection and action makes July a powerful and transformative month.

## *Work*

July emphasizes balance and strategic planning in Capricorn's professional life.

- **Opportunities:** Cancer energy supports strengthening workplace relationships and focusing on long-term career goals. Late in the month, Leo's influence inspires confidence, creativity, and leadership, making it a great time to pitch ideas or take on challenging projects.
- **Challenges:** Managing your emotions while navigating professional demands may feel challenging. Avoid letting personal concerns interfere with work performance.

**Advice:** Use Cancer's reflective energy to align your professional actions with your values and Leo's boldness to execute them effectively.

## _Finance_

Your financial outlook in July highlights thoughtful planning and cautious spending.

- **Opportunities:** Financial gains may come from collaborative efforts, bonuses, or the results of past investments. Late in the month, creative projects or leadership roles may bring additional rewards.
- **Challenges:** Avoid impulsive spending, especially during moments of emotional highs or lows.

**Advice:** Focus on saving and aligning your financial decisions with your long-term goals. Consider seeking professional advice for major investments or new ventures.

## _Love_

July brings warmth and emotional depth to Capricorn's love life.

- **For Singles:** Romantic opportunities may arise through shared interests, social gatherings, or introspective moments. Cancer's influence encourages meaningful connections, while Leo's energy later in the month adds excitement and charm to your interactions.

- **For Those in Relationships:** Focus on building trust, resolving misunderstandings, and creating memorable experiences with your partner. Late July is perfect for reigniting passion and celebrating your bond.

**Advice:** Be open and attentive in your relationships. Use Cancer energy to deepen emotional connections and Leo energy to keep things vibrant and engaging.

### *Health*

Health-wise, July encourages Capricorn to focus on emotional well-being and maintaining physical vitality.

- **Strengths:** Cancer energy supports self-care practices like journaling, meditation, or spending time in nature to nurture emotional health. Leo's influence later in the month boosts physical energy, making it a great time for outdoor activities or fitness routines.
- **Challenges:** Emotional stress or overexertion may affect your energy levels if not managed effectively.

**Advice:** Incorporate relaxation techniques into your daily routine. Focus on maintaining a balanced diet, staying hydrated, and ensuring you get adequate rest to recharge.

## *Be Careful*

- **Emotional Sensitivity:** Avoid letting strong emotions cloud your judgment in personal or professional matters.
- **Overcommitment:** Don't take on more than you can handle, as this could lead to stress or burnout.
- **Impulsiveness:** Think carefully before making significant decisions, especially in financial or personal matters.

## *Advice*

1. **Prioritize Emotional Growth:** Use Cancer's energy to nurture meaningful relationships and align with your inner self.
2. **Embrace Creativity:** As Leo season begins, take bold steps toward expressing your unique talents and ambitions.

**Balance is Key:** Maintain harmony between introspection and action to create a fulfilling and productive month.

<u>***Additional Tips***</u>

- **Lucky Days:** July 9, 18, and 28 – Ideal for decision-making, creative projects, or strengthening relationships.
- **Lucky Color:** Rose Gold – This color symbolizes warmth, vitality, and emotional balance.
- **Affirmation for July:** *"I nurture my inner self and express my creativity, creating harmony and success in my life."*

July 2025 is a month of emotional connection and creative inspiration for Capricorn. By focusing on meaningful relationships, thoughtful planning, and self-care, you'll navigate this transformative period with confidence and clarity.

# August

August 2025 is a month of ambition, transformation, and self-expression for Capricorn. With the Sun in Leo for most of the month, the focus is on stepping into leadership roles, pursuing creative projects, and embracing your confidence. As the Sun transitions into Virgo later in August, the energy shifts toward discipline, organization, and refining your long-term plans. This blend of bold energy and practicality makes August a powerful month for achieving your goals and aligning your actions with your values.

## *Work*

August emphasizes leadership and precision in Capricorn's professional life.

- **Opportunities:** Leo's dynamic energy supports showcasing your talents, pursuing bold career moves, and taking charge of important projects. Later in the month, Virgo's influence helps you refine details and ensure your efforts are sustainable.
- **Challenges:** Avoid letting pride or overconfidence lead to unnecessary risks or conflicts at work. Balance boldness with practicality.

**Advice:** Use Leo's charisma to make an impact and Virgo's grounded energy to create lasting results.

## *Finance*

Your financial outlook in August highlights growth and careful planning.

- **Opportunities:** Financial rewards may come from promotions, leadership roles, or creative endeavors. This is also a favorable time to revisit your financial goals and adjust your budget for future stability.
- **Challenges:** Avoid impulsive spending on luxuries or unnecessary items, particularly during moments of high energy or excitement.

**Advice:** Focus on saving and aligning your financial decisions with your long-term priorities. Seek advice before committing to major investments or purchases.

## *Love*

August brings passion and excitement to Capricorn's love life.

- **For Singles:** Romantic opportunities may arise through social events, creative pursuits, or professional connections. Leo's influence boosts your charm and confidence, making it an excellent time to meet new people.

- **For Those in Relationships:** Focus on rekindling passion and celebrating your bond with your partner. Late August is ideal for having meaningful discussions about your shared goals and nurturing stability.

**Advice:** Be open and expressive in your relationships. Use Leo's bold energy to keep things exciting and Virgo's practicality to build trust and understanding.

## *Health*

Health-wise, August encourages Capricorn to balance energy and maintain consistency in self-care.

- **Strengths:** Leo's energy inspires physical activity and motivation, making it a great time to engage in fitness routines or outdoor adventures. Virgo's influence later in the month promotes discipline and healthy habits.
- **Challenges:** Overexertion or neglecting rest during Leo's busy energy may lead to fatigue if not managed properly.

**Advice:** Incorporate both dynamic exercise and calming practices like yoga or meditation into your routine.

Focus on balanced nutrition and staying hydrated to sustain your vitality.

## *Be Careful*

- **Overconfidence:** Avoid taking unnecessary risks or making hasty decisions in financial or professional matters.
- **Burnout:** Don't overcommit responsibilities or neglect downtime, as this could lead to stress.
- **Neglecting Details:** While focusing on big-picture goals, ensure you're addressing important specifics, especially as Virgo season begins.

## *Advice*

1. **Step into Leadership:** Use Leo's energy to showcase your talents, take bold steps, and embrace your unique strengths.
2. **Refine and Organize:** As Virgo season begins, focus on aligning your actions with your long-term vision and creating sustainable plans.
3. **Balance is Key:** Maintain harmony by prioritizing both ambition and self-care to sustain your energy and focus.

<u>*Additional Tips*</u>

- **Lucky Days:** August 7, 15, and 26 – Ideal for decision-making, creative projects, or strengthening relationships.
- **Lucky Color:** Gold – This color symbolizes confidence, vitality, and success.
- **Affirmation for August:** *"I embrace my ambition and align my actions with purpose, creating harmony and success in all areas of my life."*

August 2025 is a month of confidence and productivity for Capricorn. By focusing on ambitious goals, meaningful connections, and disciplined planning, you'll make the most of this dynamic and fulfilling period.

# September

September 2025 is a month of focus, precision, and steady progress for Capricorn. With the Sun in Virgo for most of the month, the energy supports organizing your goals, refining your plans, and focusing on long-term stability. As the Sun transitions into Libra later in September, the focus shifts to balance, collaboration, and fostering meaningful relationships. This blend of grounded effort and harmonious connection makes September a productive and fulfilling time for Capricorn.

## *Work*

September emphasizes discipline and teamwork in Capricorn's professional life.

- **Opportunities:** Virgo Energy supports completing detailed tasks, improving processes, and laying the groundwork for major projects. Late in the month, Libra's influence encourages collaboration, networking, and building positive workplace relationships.
- **Challenges:** Avoid being overly critical of yourself or others. Perfectionism may slow your progress if left unchecked.

**Advice:** Use Virgo's meticulous energy to refine your plans and Libra's diplomacy to foster collaboration and explore creative solutions.

## _Finance_

Your financial outlook in September highlights stability and careful management.

- **Opportunities:** Financial rewards may come from disciplined budgeting, investments, or successful long-term planning. This is a favorable time to reassess your financial goals and prioritize savings.
- **Challenges:** Avoid overanalyzing financial decisions or spending on unnecessary items during moments of indulgence.

**Advice:** Stick to a practical budget and focus on building financial security. Seek advice if considering new investments or significant financial changes.

## _Love_

September brings warmth and connection to Capricorn's love life, with Venus enhancing harmony and emotional depth.

- **For Singles:** Romantic opportunities may arise through work, shared activities, or intellectual pursuits. Virgo energy encourages meaningful connections based on shared values, while Libra's charm later in the month brings excitement and balance.

- **For Those in Relationships:** Focus on deepening emotional intimacy and nurturing stability in your relationship. Late September is ideal for planning quality time together or resolving conflicts with compassion.

**Advice:** Be open and genuine in your interactions. Use Virgo's grounding influence to build trust and Libra's charm to keep the connection fresh and harmonious.

### *Health*

Health-wise, September encourages Capricorn to maintain discipline and consistency in wellness routines.

- **Strengths:** Virgo Energy supports grounding practices like yoga, mindfulness, or regular exercise that enhance physical and mental well-being. Libra's influence later in the month promotes activities that balance both body and mind.
- **Challenges:** Stress from overworking or neglecting rest may affect your energy levels if not managed carefully.

**Advice:** Focus on a balanced diet, regular hydration, and incorporating relaxation techniques into your routine. Prioritize rest to recharge.

## *Be Careful*

- **Overthinking:** Avoid becoming overly critical or bogged down by details, especially in work or personal relationships.
- **Impatience:** Balance your drive for perfection with realistic timelines to avoid frustration.
- **Neglecting Balance:** Ensure you're giving equal attention to work, relationships, and self-care.

## *Advice*

1. **Refine Your Goals:** Use Virgo energy to organize and align your efforts with your long-term vision.
2. **Foster Relationships:** Embrace Libra's influence to build harmony and strengthen meaningful connections.
3. **Prioritize Balance:** Maintain harmony by dedicating time to both productivity and relaxation.

## *Additional Tips*

- **Lucky Days:** September 10, 18, and 28 – Ideal for decision-making, networking, or creative pursuits.

- **Lucky Color:** Forest Green – This color symbolizes growth, balance, and renewal.
- **Affirmation for September:** *"I align my actions with my goals, creating harmony and success in all areas of my life."*

September 2025 is a month of thoughtful planning and meaningful progress for Capricorn. By focusing on refining your goals, nurturing relationships, and maintaining balance, you'll navigate this productive period with confidence and clarity.

# October

October 2025 is a month of balance, connection, and forward planning for Capricorn. With the Sun in Libra for most of the month, the energy supports fostering relationships, collaboration, and finding harmony in your personal and professional life. As the Sun transitions into Scorpio later in October, the focus shifts to transformation, deeper introspection, and aligning with your long-term goals. This blend of social engagement and inner focus makes October a powerful and transformative time.

## *Work*

October emphasizes teamwork and strategic decision-making in Capricorn's professional life.

- **Opportunities:** Libra Energy supports networking, building alliances, and resolving workplace dynamics with diplomacy. Late in the month, Scorpio's influence encourages tackling complex projects, focusing on long-term strategies, and addressing challenges with determination.
- **Challenges:** Avoid indecision or overcomplicating matters during Libra season. Balance social engagement with the need for individual focus.

**Advice:** Use Libra's charm to strengthen professional relationships and Scorpio's intensity to deepen your focus and drive.

### *Finance*

Your financial outlook in October highlights stability and preparation.

- **Opportunities:** Financial rewards may come from partnerships, collaborative efforts, or bonuses for past projects. This is also a favorable time to evaluate your budget and align your financial decisions with your future goals.
- **Challenges:** Avoid impulsive spending during moments of indulgence or emotional highs.

**Advice:** Focus on financial discipline and saving for long-term priorities. Seek advice before making major investments or financial commitments.

### *Love*

October brings warmth and depth to Capricorn's love life, with Venus enhancing connection and emotional intimacy.

- **For Singles:** Romantic opportunities may arise through social gatherings, mutual connections, or intellectual pursuits. Libra's influence encourages lighthearted connections, while Scorpio's energy later in the month adds passion and emotional depth.

- **For Those in Relationships:** Focus on nurturing trust and resolving conflicts with your partner. Late October is perfect for reigniting passion and strengthening your bond through shared experiences.

**Advice:** Be open and attentive in your interactions. Use Libra's diplomacy to maintain harmony and Scorpio's intensity to deepen intimacy.

## *Health*

Health-wise, October encourages Capricorn to prioritize balance and emotional well-being.

- **Strengths:** Libra energy supports engaging in group fitness activities or mindfulness practices that enhance relaxation and connection. Scorpio's influence later in the month inspires transformative habits for long-term wellness.
- **Challenges:** Stress from juggling responsibilities or neglecting self-care may affect your energy levels if not managed properly.

**Advice:** Maintain a consistent wellness routine that includes both physical activity and mental relaxation.

Focus on a balanced diet, staying hydrated, and getting enough rest.

## *Be Careful*

- **Indecision:** Avoid procrastinating or overthinking decisions in work or personal matters. Trust your instincts and take action when needed.
- **Overcommitting:** Don't take on too many responsibilities, as this could lead to stress or burnout.
- **Emotional Sensitivity:** Practice mindfulness to manage strong emotions and avoid misunderstandings in relationships.

## *Advice*

1. **Build Connections:** Use Libra's influence to nurture relationships and collaborate effectively.
2. **Embrace Transformation:** As Scorpio season begins, focus on aligning your goals with your values and embracing meaningful change.
3. **Prioritize Self-Care:** Balance your active lifestyle with relaxation and mindfulness to sustain your energy and clarity.

<u>*Additional Tips*</u>

- **Lucky Days:** October 9, 17, and 28 — Ideal for decision-making, creative pursuits, or strengthening relationships.
- **Lucky Color:** Deep Maroon — This color symbolizes resilience, passion, and transformation.
- **Affirmation for October:** *"I balance connection with introspection, creating harmony and growth in all areas of my life."*

October 2025 is a month of dynamic energy and meaningful progress for Capricorn. By focusing on relationships, thoughtful planning, and self-care, you'll navigate this transformative period with confidence and clarity.

# November

November 2025 is a month of introspection, transformation, and progress for Capricorn. With the Sun in Scorpio for most of the month, the energy supports deep reflection, tackling complex challenges, and aligning your goals with your inner values. As the Sun transitions into Sagittarius later in November, the focus shifts to exploration, optimism, and planning. This blend of emotional depth and adventurous energy makes November a powerful and inspiring time.

## *Work*

November emphasizes focus and transformation in Capricorn's professional life.

- **Opportunities:** Scorpio Energy supports addressing long-term challenges, refining your strategies, and diving deep into projects requiring focus and perseverance. Late in the month, Sagittarius' influence encourages dynamic thinking, networking, and exploring new opportunities.
- **Challenges:** Avoid overanalyzing or hesitating to make bold moves, particularly during moments of uncertainty. Trust your instincts and act with clarity.

**Advice:** Use Scorpio's energy to refine your plans and Sagittarius' optimism to take bold steps toward your goals.

## *Finance*

Your financial outlook in November highlights planning and potential growth.

- **Opportunities:** Financial gains may come from investments, bonuses, or successful completion of long-term projects. Late in the month, Sagittarius Energy inspires the exploration of new income streams or financial strategies.
- **Challenges:** Avoid impulsive spending or risky investments, particularly during moments of high enthusiasm.

**Advice:** Stick to a disciplined budget and focus on aligning financial decisions with your long-term priorities. Seek advice before making significant financial commitments.

## *Love*

November brings passion and an emotional connection to Capricorn's love life.

- **For Singles:** Romantic opportunities may arise through introspective activities, mutual connections, or shared interests. Scorpio energy enhances emotional intensity and compatibility, while Sagittarius' influence later in the month adds excitement and charm.

- **For Those in Relationships:** Focus on building trust, resolving conflicts, and deepening emotional intimacy with your partner. Late November is ideal for planning adventures or exploring new aspects of your relationship.

**Advice:** Be open and present in your relationships. Use Scorpio energy to nurture emotional bonds and Sagittarius energy to keep the connection lively and engaging.

## *Health*

Health-wise, November encourages Capricorn to focus on emotional resilience and physical vitality.

- **Strengths:** Scorpio Energy supports transformative habits like detoxifying routines, meditation, or journaling. Late in the month, Sagittarius energy boosts motivation for outdoor activities and fitness goals.
- **Challenges:** Stress or emotional intensity may affect your energy levels if not managed properly.

**Advice:** Incorporate relaxation techniques and maintain consistency in your wellness routines. Prioritize rest, hydration, and a balanced diet to sustain your energy.

## *Be Careful*

- **Emotional Intensity:** Avoid letting strong emotions cloud your judgment in personal or professional matters. Practice mindfulness and patience.
- **Overconfidence:** During Sagittarius season, be mindful of taking calculated risks rather than acting impulsively.
- **Neglecting Details:** Balance your big-picture focus with attention to finer points, particularly in financial or professional matters.

## *Advice*

1. **Reflect and Realign:** Use Scorpio's energy to assess your goals and align your actions with your deeper values.
2. **Embrace Optimism:** As Sagittarius season begins, step into your power with confidence and explore dynamic opportunities.
3. **Maintain Balance:** Prioritize self-care and meaningful connections to sustain your energy and focus.

- **Lucky Days:** November 8, 16, and 26 – Ideal for decision-making, networking, or strengthening relationships.
- **Lucky Color:** Deep Purple – This color symbolizes transformation, intuition, and resilience.
- **Affirmation for November:** *"I embrace transformation and align my actions with my purpose, creating harmony and success in my life."*

November 2025 is a month of deep reflection and dynamic progress for Capricorn. By focusing on personal growth, meaningful relationships, and thoughtful planning, you'll navigate this transformative period with clarity and confidence.

## December

December 2025 is a month of celebration, focus, and preparation for Capricorn. With the Sun in Sagittarius for most of the month, the energy supports exploration, setting new goals, and expanding your vision. As the Sun transitions into your sign later in December, you'll feel a surge of confidence, clarity, and determination to take charge of your ambitions. This blend of optimism and grounded energy makes December a powerful time for closing the year on a high note and setting the stage for success in 2026.

## *Work*

December emphasizes planning and bold action in Capricorn's professional life.

- **Opportunities:** Sagittarius Energy supports brainstorming new ideas, networking, and exploring innovative approaches to your career. Late in the month, Capricorn Energy encourages refining strategies, organizing your plans, and laying the foundation for long-term success.
- **Challenges:** Balancing your enthusiasm with the need for discipline and consistency may feel challenging during Sagittarius season.

**Advice:** Use Sagittarius energy to dream big and Capricorn energy to focus on actionable steps that align with your goals.

## *Finance*

Your financial outlook in December highlights stability and growth.

- **Opportunities:** Financial rewards may come from bonuses, year-end incentives, or investments that have matured. This is also a favorable time to review your financial goals and plan for major expenses in 2026.
- **Challenges:** Avoid overspending on holiday-related expenses or indulging in impulsive purchases.

**Advice:** Stick to a disciplined budget and focus on saving for future goals while enjoying the festive season responsibly.

## *Love*

December brings warmth and connection to Capricorn's love life.

- **For Singles:** Romantic opportunities may arise through social events, travel, or shared interests. Sagittarius energy encourages lighthearted and exciting connections, while Capricorn's influence later in the month deepens emotional bonds.

- **For Those in Relationships:** Focus on celebrating your bond with your partner through thoughtful gestures, shared adventures, and meaningful conversations. Late December is ideal for discussing long-term plans and strengthening your commitment.

**Advice:** Be open and expressive in your relationships. Use Sagittarius energy to keep things lively and Capricorn energy to nurture stability and trust.

## *Health*

Health-wise, December encourages Capricorn to maintain balance and focus on well-being.

- **Strengths:** Sagittarius energy supports physical activity and exploring new fitness routines, while Capricorn's influence inspires consistency and discipline.
- **Challenges:** Overindulgence in food, drinks, or social activities during the festive season may affect your energy if not managed properly.

**Advice:** Practice moderation, maintain a balanced diet, and prioritize self-care. Incorporate relaxation techniques into your routine to stay grounded and energized.

## *Be Careful*

- **Overspending:** Avoid exceeding your budget on gifts, travel, or celebrations. Stick to a financial plan that prioritizes long-term stability.
- **Burnout:** Balance social activities with rest to avoid overstretching yourself during the busy holiday season.
- **Neglecting Self-Care:** Don't let the festive excitement distract you from your wellness routines.

## *Advice*

1. **Celebrate and Reflect:** Use Sagittarius energy to celebrate your accomplishments and reflect on the year's journey.
2. **Plan Strategically:** Embrace Capricorn's influence to set clear and achievable goals for the upcoming year.
3. **Nurture Connections:** Strengthen bonds with loved ones by expressing gratitude and sharing meaningful moments.

- **Lucky Days:** December 7, 14, and 30 – Perfect for decision-making, creative pursuits, or building relationships.
- **Lucky Color:** Midnight Blue – This color symbolizes wisdom, clarity, and strength.
- **Affirmation for December:** *"I celebrate my journey and align my goals with purpose, creating harmony and success in all areas of my life."*

December 2025 is a month of celebration and preparation for Capricorn. By focusing on meaningful connections, disciplined planning, and self-care, you'll close the year with a sense of fulfillment and set the stage for a prosperous 2026.

# Good Luck
# For
# 2025